Dinosaurs

ISBN 1-74089-368-9
Colour reproduction by
Colourscan Overseas Co Pte Ltd
Printed by SNP Leefung Printers

Printed in China

Dinosaurs

CONSULTING EDITOR

Dr Angela Milner

Head of the Fossil Vertebrates and Anthropology Division
Natural History Museum, London, England

WELDON OWEN

Contents

• THE ARRIVAL OF THE DINOSAURS •

• A PARADE OF DINOSAURS •

Blue-green algae and bacteria

Soft-bodied organisms
Fossils of algae, bacteria and jellyfish are rare. Their soft bodies usually rotted quickly, before mud could harden on them.

Animals with shells
Between 590 and 250 million years ago, there were more than 10,000 kinds of trilobites. They ranged from 3 cm (1 in) to 50 cm (1½ ft) in length.

Jellyfish

Ammonite

Trilobites

Pteraspis

Drepanaspis

Scorpion

Before the Dinosaurs

The Earth began 4,600 million years ago. Its long history is divided into different periods, during which an amazing variety of life forms developed or died out. In the beginning, single-celled algae and bacteria formed, or evolved, in the warm seas that covered most of the planet.

In the Palaeozoic Era, more complex plants and animals appeared in the sea: worms, jellyfish and hard-shelled molluscs swarmed in shallow waters and were eaten by bony fish. When plants and animals first appeared on land, they were eaten by amphibians that had evolved from fish with lungs and strong fins. Some amphibians then evolved into reptiles that did not lay their eggs in water. Early reptiles developed into turtles and tortoises, lizards, crocodiles, birds, and the first dinosaurs. They dominated the world for millions of years.

The first jawless fish
Armour-plated fish such as *Pteraspis* and *Drepanaspis* did not have jaws. They sucked up food from the mud or fed on plankton.

A bony fish
Dunkleosteus, a giant of late Devonian seas, grew to 3.4 m (11 feet). It grasped its prey in sharp, bony dental plates because it did not have teeth.

An amphibian
Ichthyostega could not expand or contract its solid rib cage. This 1-m (3-ft) long amphibian had to use its mouth to push air into its lungs.

An early reptile
Hylonomus, a 20-cm (8-in) long reptile, is known only from fossils found in the remains of hollow tree trunks, where it may have become trapped while hunting insects.

A mammal-like reptile
Dimetrodon, which was 3 m (10 ft) long, may have angled its "sail" to catch sunlight so that it could warm up quickly in the morning.

Thecodontian archosaurs
Ornithosuchus looked like *Tyrannosaurus*, but it was not a dinosaur. It had five toes on each hind foot while *Tyrannosaurus* had only three.

THE DINOSAUR RACE

Dinosaurs, which appeared in the Triassic Period, were descended from crocodile-like reptiles, whose legs sprawled at right angles from their bodies. *Euparkeria*, from the early Triassic Period, had straighter legs and carried its body off the ground. The legs of *Lagosuchus*, from the middle Triassic Period, were tucked beneath its body and it walked on its hind legs. By the late Triassic Period, the predator *Ornithosuchus* looked a little like a dinosaur, but the earliest known dinosaur was *Eoraptor*. It appeared 228 million years ago.

Ornithosuchus
4 m (13 ft)

Euparkeria
60 cm (2 ft)

Lagosuchus
30 cm (1 ft)

Eoraptor
1.2 m (4 ft)

	millions of years ago	4,600	2,500	570	510	439	408	362	290	245
Origin of the Earth		Precambrian Era		Palaeozoic Era						
		Archaean	Proterozoic	Cambrian	Ordovician	Silurian	Devonian	Carboniferous	Permian	
		First algae and single-celled bacteria appeared in the seas.	First animals with soft bodies and many cells. They looked like worms and jellyfish.	First sponges, segmented worms and hard-shelled animals.	First animals with backbones; jawless fish, then sharks and bony fish.	First land plants. Sea scorpions up to 2 m (7 ft) dominated the seas.	The Age of Fishes and the first land animals with backbones.	The Age of Amphibians. Primitive reptiles hunted insects and small amphibians.	Many species of reptiles that ate plants and meat. Trilobites disappear.	

Dunkleosteus

Ichthyostega

Dimetrodon

Dragonfly

Hylonomus

Ornithosuchus

What is a dinosaur?

Dinosaurs were very special reptiles. Some were the size of chickens; others may have been as long as jumbo jets. These creatures were the most successful animals that have ever lived on Earth. They dominated the world for nearly 150 million years and were found on every continent during the Mesozoic Era, which is divided into the Triassic, Jurassic and Cretaceous periods. Like reptiles today, dinosaurs had scaly skin and laid their eggs in shells. The earliest dinosaurs ate meat, while later plant-eating dinosaurs enjoyed the lush plant life around them. Dinosaurs are called "lizard-hipped" or "bird-hipped", depending on how their hip bones were arranged. They stood on either four legs or two, and walked with straight legs tucked beneath their bodies. Dinosaurs are the only reptiles that have ever been able to do this.

JURASSIC HUNTERS
In a scene from the Jurassic Period in North America, 21-m (69-ft) long *Apatosaurus* munches on a cycad as a 2-m (7-ft) long *Ornitholestes* pounces on a salamander disturbed by the browsing giant.

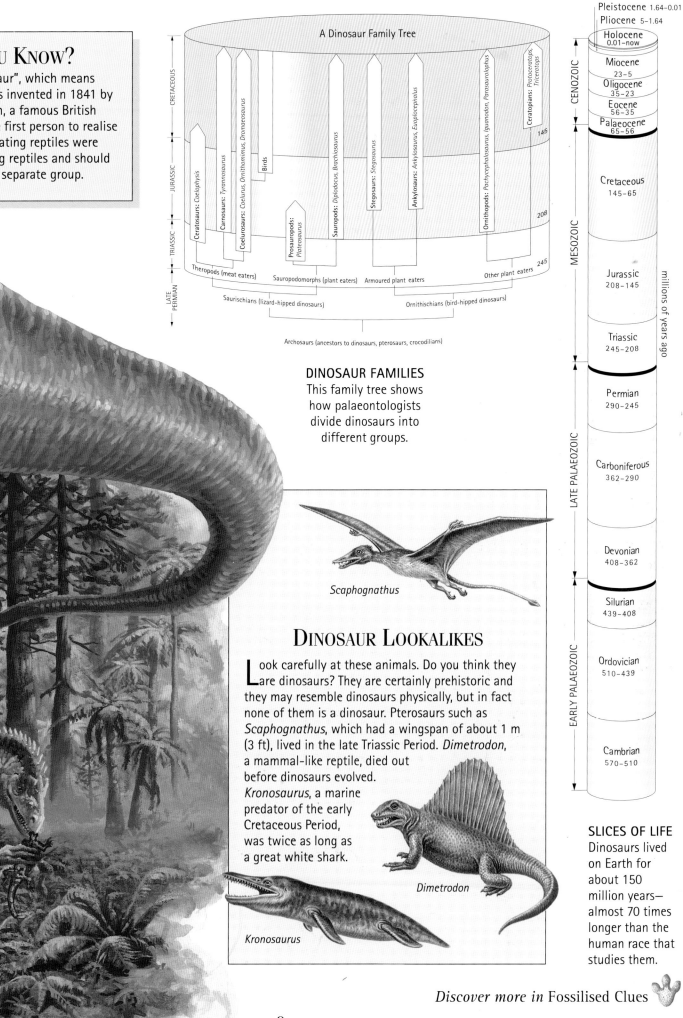

A Dinosaur Family Tree

CRETACEOUS — JURASSIC — TRIASSIC — LATE PERMIAN

145

208

245

Ceratosaurs: *Coelophysis*
Carnosaurs: *Tyrannosaurus*
Coelurosaurs: *Coelurus, Ornithomimus, Dromaeosaurus*
Birds
Prosauropods: *Plateosaurus*
Sauropods: *Diplodocus, Brachiosaurus*
Stegosaurs: *Stegosaurus*
Ankylosaurs: *Ankylosaurus, Euoplocephalus*
Ornithopods: *Pachycephalosaurus, Iguanodon, Parasaurolophus*
Ceratopians: *Protoceratops, Triceratops*

Theropods (meat eaters)   Sauropodomorphs (plant eaters)   Armoured plant eaters   Other plant eaters

Saurischians (lizard-hipped dinosaurs)   Ornithischians (bird-hipped dinosaurs)

Archosaurs (ancestors to dinosaurs, pterosaurs, crocodilians)

DINOSAUR FAMILIES

This family tree shows how palaeontologists divide dinosaurs into different groups.

Scaphognathus

DINOSAUR LOOKALIKES

Look carefully at these animals. Do you think they are dinosaurs? They are certainly prehistoric and they may resemble dinosaurs physically, but in fact none of them is a dinosaur. Pterosaurs such as *Scaphognathus*, which had a wingspan of about 1 m (3 ft), lived in the late Triassic Period. *Dimetrodon*, a mammal-like reptile, died out before dinosaurs evolved. *Kronosaurus*, a marine predator of the early Cretaceous Period, was twice as long as a great white shark.

Dimetrodon

Kronosaurus

Pleistocene 1.64–0.01
Pliocene 5–1.64
Holocene 0.01–now
Miocene 23–5
Oligocene 35–23
Eocene 56–35
Palaeocene 65–56

CENOZOIC

Cretaceous 145–65

Jurassic 208–145

Triassic 245–208

MESOZOIC

millions of years ago

Permian 290–245

Carboniferous 362–290

Devonian 408–362

LATE PALAEOZOIC

Silurian 439–408

Ordovician 510–439

Cambrian 570–510

EARLY PALAEOZOIC

SLICES OF LIFE

Dinosaurs lived on Earth for about 150 million years— almost 70 times longer than the human race that studies them.

Discover more in Fossilised Clues

SPRAWLING
The ancestors of the dinosaurs sprawled on four legs, like a lizard. They had to use large amounts of energy to twist the whole body and lift each leg in turn.

HALFWAY UP
Some reptiles, such as crocodiles, have upright hind legs. As their bodies are off the ground, they can run on their hind legs for short distances.

ON TWO LEGS
A dinosaur's weight was supported easily by its straight legs, tucked under its body. As the body weight was balanced over the hips by the weight of the tail, some dinosaurs were bipedal (two-legged) and used their hands for grasping.

TWO-LEGGED PLANT EATER
This 13-m (43-ft) long *Edmontosaurus* has a typical ornithischian pelvis. The pubis points backwards and allows more space for the large intestines that plant eaters needed to digest their food. In sauropods (plant-eating saurischians) the intestines are slung forward. This means that the forward-pointing pubis does not get in the way of these four-legged (quadrupedal) dinosaurs.

Dinosaur Hips

Dinosaurs walked upright with their legs beneath their bodies. No other reptiles have been able to do this. Dinosaurs had a right-angled joint at the top of the leg bone that fitted into a hole in the hip bones. This allowed the limbs to be positioned under the body, so the weight of the dinosaur was supported, and all the joints worked as simple forward and backward hinges. These evolutionary advances were the key to the great success of the dinosaurs. They did not have to throw the whole body from side to side to move their legs, so they could breathe easily while running quickly. They were able to grow bigger, walk further and move faster than any other reptiles. The two main groups of dinosaurs had different kinds of hips. The meat eaters and plant-eating sauropods (called saurischians, or lizard-hipped dinosaurs) had a forward-pointing pubis. In the plant-eating ornithischians, or bird-hipped dinosaurs, part of the pubis pointed backward, to allow more space for the gut.

Ilium

Pubis

Ischium

Ornithischian hip

EVOLVING SIDE BY SIDE

Alligator

Some dinosaurs were called "bird-hipped", but this does not mean that birds have the same kinds of hips as these dinosaurs, even though their hips look similar. A bird walks on its hind legs, with its body tipped forward and supported in the same way as two-legged dinosaurs. Birds, however, actually evolved from lizard-hipped dinosaurs. An alligator's hip bones look similar to those of a lizard-hipped dinosaur because they had common ancestors.

Starling

STRANGE BUT TRUE

Fossils sometimes reveal illnesses, accidents and injuries. Sometime in the early Cretaceous Period, an *Iguanodon* fractured its hip. The dinosaur recovered, but was left with a bulge of new bone around the fracture.

Healed fracture

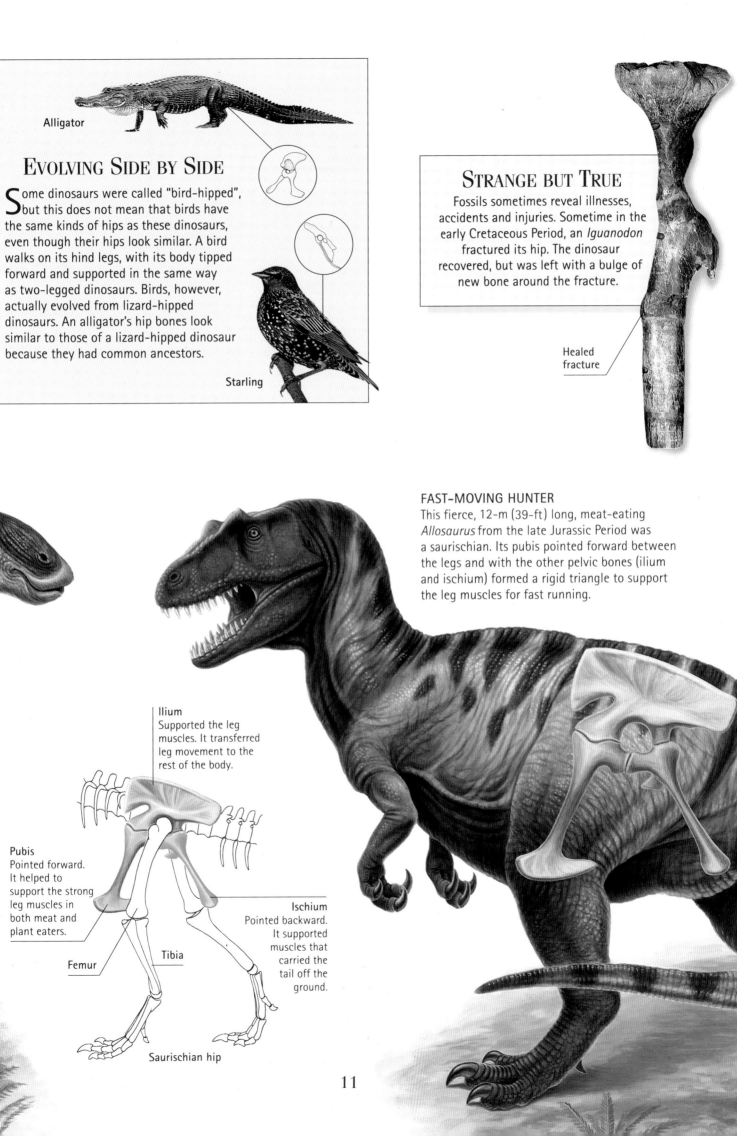

FAST-MOVING HUNTER
This fierce, 12-m (39-ft) long, meat-eating *Allosaurus* from the late Jurassic Period was a saurischian. Its pubis pointed forward between the legs and with the other pelvic bones (ilium and ischium) formed a rigid triangle to support the leg muscles for fast running.

Ilium
Supported the leg muscles. It transferred leg movement to the rest of the body.

Pubis
Pointed forward. It helped to support the strong leg muscles in both meat and plant eaters.

Ischium
Pointed backward. It supported muscles that carried the tail off the ground.

Femur

Tibia

Saurischian hip

11

Longest-winged pterosaur
Pteranodon had a long, toothless beak. It probably scooped up fish in its narrow jaws, just like a pelican.

Fish eater
Dimorphodon, a pterosaur, had a long tail and forward-facing teeth to grasp its prey.

Pint-sized flier
Archaeopteryx, the earliest bird of all, evolved from the dinosaurs. It probably ate insects and small reptiles.

TARGET IN SIGHT
Above the seas in the late Jurassic Period, one of the most common pterosaurs, *Rhamphorhynchus*, spies *Muraenosaurus*, a 6-m (20-ft) long plesiosaur, attacking a school of *Leptolepis* fish. *Rhamphorhynchus* had a leaf-shaped membrane on the end of its tail to help it steer in flight.

In the Sea and in the Air

During the Mesozoic Era, dinosaurs ruled the land, marine reptiles dominated the sea and flying reptiles, called pterosaurs, glided through the skies. Marine reptiles and pterosaurs were only distant cousins of the dinosaurs, even though some marine reptiles looked almost like long-necked sauropods with fins. Pterosaurs were the first animals with backbones to take to the air—on wings made of skin. Many of them hunted fish, but others such as *Quetzalcoatlus*, the largest flying animal of all time, had no teeth, and used its jaws to eat decaying animals. Plesiosaurs, pliosaurs, marine turtles, crocodiles and other sea reptiles lived in the waters of the Mesozoic world. The plesiosaurs had long necks and ate small sea creatures, while the big-headed, short-necked pliosaurs tackled larger prey with their strong teeth and jaws.

WORLDS APART

There were differences among the flying animals of the Mesozoic Era—differences that can still be seen in flying creatures today. The wings of a pterosaur were skin membranes, supported by a long fourth finger. The wings of a living bat are also made of skin membrane. However, a bat's wings are supported by all its fingers. Modern birds evolved from *Archaeopteryx*. Its wings were made of feathers that were arranged in a similar way to those of a living bird, such as a pigeon.

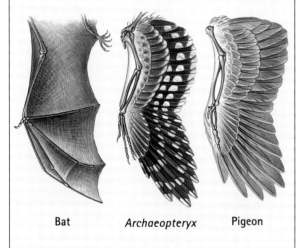

Bat   *Archaeopteryx*   Pigeon

FISHY LIZARD

Ichthyosaurus (meaning "fish-lizard") was about 2 m (7 ft) long, with a streamlined body shaped like a dolphin. Palaeontologists think it could reach a speed of 40 km (25 miles) per hour for short bursts.

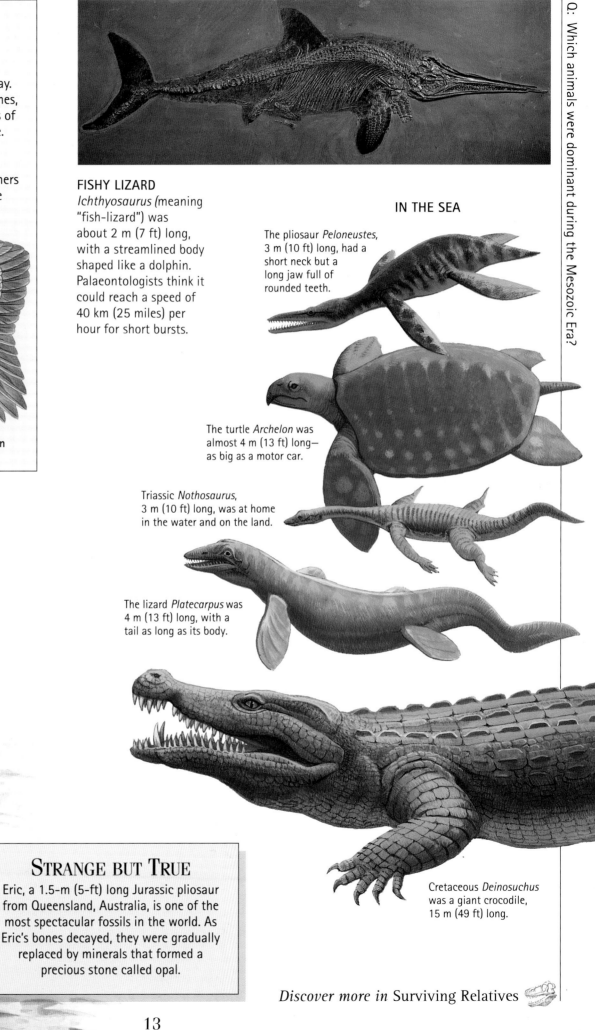

IN THE SEA

The pliosaur *Peloneustes*, 3 m (10 ft) long, had a short neck but a long jaw full of rounded teeth.

The turtle *Archelon* was almost 4 m (13 ft) long— as big as a motor car.

Triassic *Nothosaurus*, 3 m (10 ft) long, was at home in the water and on the land.

The lizard *Platecarpus* was 4 m (13 ft) long, with a tail as long as its body.

Cretaceous *Deinosuchus* was a giant crocodile, 15 m (49 ft) long.

STRANGE BUT TRUE

Eric, a 1.5-m (5-ft) long Jurassic pliosaur from Queensland, Australia, is one of the most spectacular fossils in the world. As Eric's bones decayed, they were gradually replaced by minerals that formed a precious stone called opal.

Discover more in Surviving Relatives

A VIEW OF THE WORLD

In the Triassic Period, the continents fitted together into one huge continent called Pangaea. Fossils show that most dinosaurs lived near the centre of Pangaea, the area now divided among North America, Africa and northern Europe.

Ginkgo tree

FOSSIL SITES OF TRIASSIC DINOSAURS

• THE ARRIVAL OF THE DINOSAURS •

The Triassic World

The Triassic Period was the "Dawn of the Dinosaurs". The Earth was a huge supercontinent called Pangaea (from the Greek meaning "all Earth"), which had three main environments and was dominated by mammal-like reptiles. Near the coasts, forests of giant horsetail ferns, tree ferns and ginkgo trees were alive with insects; amphibians; small reptiles, such as the first turtles, lizards and crocodiles; and early mammals. The dry, cool areas near the equator had forests of tall conifers (pine and fir trees) and palmlike cycads. The centre of Pangaea was covered by hot, sandy deserts. Many different plants and animals developed in these varied climates. There was plenty of food for many life forms, especially one group of animals that first appeared 228 million years ago—the dinosaurs. These extraordinary creatures began to rule the Triassic world.

Coelophysis

THE CHASE
In the warm, moist forest close to the coast of Pangaea, two *Coelophysis* chase a *Planocephalosaurus* up a tree.

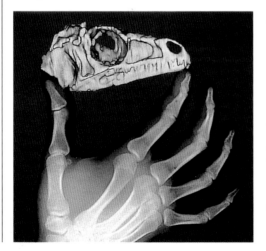

AN EARLY DINOSAUR
Eoraptor, the earliest known dinosaur (a fossilised head is shown supported by a human hand), lived 228 million years ago in what is now South America. This fast, lizard-hipped animal did not have a flexible jaw, so it could not trap struggling prey. It probably scavenged food from animals killed by larger reptiles.

TRIASSIC DINOSAURS

Horsetails

Cycads

Zanclodon was a 6-m (20-ft) long, meat-eating carnosaur.

Herrerasaurus was a 3-m (10-ft) long, meat-eating coelurosaur.

Procompsognathus was a 1.2-m (4-ft) long, meat-eating coelurosaur.

Saltopus was a 60-cm (2-ft) long, meat-eating carnosaur.

Plateosaurus was an 8-m (26-ft) long, plant-eating prosauropod.

DINOSAUR DIETS

Before flowering plants appeared in the Cretaceous Period, plant-eating dinosaurs browsed on ferns and tree leaves. Many plants had tough, waxy coatings or spines to protect themselves.

Meat-eating dinosaurs such as *Eoraptor* and *Coelophysis* hunted insects such as cockroaches and dragonflies, frogs, mammal-like reptiles and even early mammals —our distant ancestors.

Dragonfly

Tree fern   *Wielandiella*   *Haramiya*

Discover more in Meat-eating Dinosaurs

15

As the two supercontinents moved apart, the centres of dinosaur evolution spread. Most of the plant-eating sauropods, for example, remained in Gondwana, but some theropods, such as *Allosaurus*, spread throughout Laurasia.

Laurasia

Gondwana

Tree ferns

FOSSIL SITES OF JURASSIC DINOSAURS

STRANGE BUT TRUE

The forests that covered the Jurassic world survive today—as seams of coal. Dead trees (even whole forests destroyed by storms or floods) were covered by mud and soil. They slowly hardened into material that looks like rock, but burns like wood!

REARING ITS HEAD
A *Diplodocus* rears to defend itself against a predator. Its clawed front feet and lashing tail are ready for battle.

• THE ARRIVAL OF THE DINOSAURS •

The Jurassic World

Towards the end of the Triassic Period, the supercontinent of Pangaea started to divide into two smaller, but still very large continents—Laurasia and Gondwana. New kinds of dinosaurs began to evolve on these new continents as they moved further apart. The slightly cooler temperatures and higher rainfall of the Jurassic world created a warm, wet climate that was ideal for reptiles. The lizard-hipped dinosaurs continued to break into the two groups that first split in the Triassic Period: the meat-eating theropods, which walked on two legs; and the plant-eating sauropods, which moved on all fours. The bird-hipped dinosaurs remained plant eaters. Giant, long-necked, plant-eating sauropods; plated, bird-hipped dinosaurs such as *Stegosaurus*; and bird-hipped plant eaters such as *Camptosaurus* were some of the mighty dinosaurs roaming the Jurassic world.

Camptosaurus, 6 m (20 ft) long, from Europe and North America

Allosaurus, 12 m (39 ft) long, from North America

Stegosaurus, 9 m (30 ft) long, from North America

Coelurus, 2 m (7 ft) long, from North America

A SIZABLE APPETITE

Brachiosaurus was 12 m (39 ft) high and 23 m (75 ft) from nose to tail. It weighed an incredible 80 tonnes (78 tons)—as much as 12 African elephants—and ate the equivalent of 35 bales of hay a day. Its front legs were longer than its hind legs and its whole body sloped downward from the shoulders (like a giraffe today), so its long neck could reach the tasty young leaves at the tops of the tallest trees.

Cycads

FOOD FOR DINOSAURS
Jurassic dinosaurs ate many animals, including freshwater turtles such as *Pleisochelys* and perhaps even the earliest bird *Archaeopteryx*.

Ground cover ferns

Discover more in Long-necked Dinosaurs

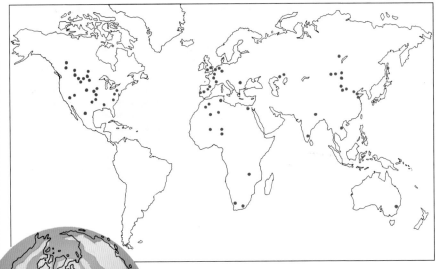

FOSSIL SITES OF CRETACEOUS DINOSAURS

MOVING CONTINENTS
Laurasia and Gondwana continued to move apart during the Cretaceous Period. By the end of this period, the outlines of the continents were roughly the same as they are today. There were land bridges between the continents, but dinosaurs tended to evolve separately on each of the landmasses.

Conifer forest

• THE ARRIVAL OF THE DINOSAURS •

The Cretaceous World

The Cretaceous Period lasted for 80 million years. More dinosaur species evolved in this time than in all the other dinosaur periods put together. But at the end of this period, about 65 million years ago, the dinosaurs disappeared. The early Cretaceous Period was warm. Winters were mild and dry, and most of the rain fell in summer. Later, summers became hotter and winters were colder in the temperate and polar regions. The giant plant eaters disappeared and were replaced by smaller species such as *Triceratops* and the duckbilled dinosaurs. Flowering plants evolved during this period (giant plant eaters during the Jurassic Period ate and trampled down so much of the vegetation that it gave new plants the chance to grow) and were eaten by hundreds of new species of plant-eating animals. There was a huge amount of food to support an enormous number of animals. The animals that ate the flowering plants were also eaten by predators, from snakes (which first appeared in this period) to great predatory dinosaurs such as *Tyrannosaurus*.

Magnolias

PREDATORS AND PREY
In this scene from the late Cretaceous Period in Mongolia, a *Velociraptor* (above right) battles with a *Protoceratops*, squashing dinosaur eggs in the process. An inquisitive *Prenocephale* looks on at the fierce encounter.

18

THE CYCLE OF LIFE

Flowering plants (**A**) were pollinated by insects (**B**), which were eaten by small mammals such as *Alphadon* (**C**), which in turn were eaten by dinosaurs such as *Dromaeosaurus* (**D**). Dinosaur droppings fertilised plants, and the cycle continued.

RELATED BUT NOT ALIKE

Animals that belong to the same family can evolve quite differently if they become isolated. *Hypacrosaurus* and *Bactrosaurus* were both duckbilled dinosaurs, and may have evolved from the same ancestor. But *Hypacrosaurus*, which lived in North America, was 9 m (30 ft) long and had a semi-circular crest on its head. *Bactrosaurus*, from central Asia, was only 4 m (13 ft) long. When the continents drifted apart, these dinosaurs evolved in different ways because they lived in such different places.

Saltasaurus

Tyrannosaurus

Triceratops

Corythosaurus

Pachycephalosaurus

Euoplocephalus

Meat-eating Dinosaurs

THE PREDATOR KING
Tyrannosaurus ("the tyrant lizard") was the largest predator ever to walk the Earth. This gigantic creature weighed more than an African elephant. Five complete specimens of *Tyrannosaurus* have been found around the world.

Many carnivorous dinosaurs were powerful, fast hunters that ate prey larger than themselves. But there were also smaller meat eaters (*Compsognathus* was no taller than a chicken) that ate eggs, insects, small reptiles and mammals. Carnosaurs, ceratosaurs and coelurosaurs, the three main groups of meat-eating dinosaurs, all had short, muscular bodies, slender arms, and low powerful tails that balanced strong back legs with birdlike feet. With large eyes and daggerlike teeth, they were formidable predators: the coelurosaur *Deinonychus* had long, slashing claws on its front legs that could rip open a victim's belly; *Megalosaurus,* a carnosaur, had powerful hinged jaws that were armed with curved, saw-edged fangs. Meat-eating dinosaurs had much larger brains than plant-eating dinosaurs. Hunting prey that was large and sometimes armoured required good vision and an ability to plan an attack.

Eye

Nostril

Teeth

A MEAT-EATER'S SKULL
Allosaurus, a 12-m (39-ft) long predator from the late Jurassic–early Cretaceous Period, weighed more than a tonne and its skull could be up to 1 m (3 ft) long. As its jaws were hinged, *Allosaurus* could swallow large pieces of flesh whole.

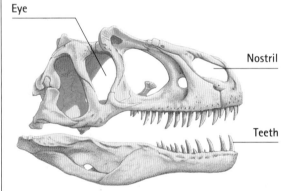

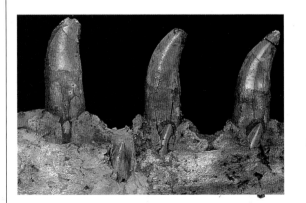

FIGHTING FOR LIFE
Tenontosaurus, a plant eater from the early Cretaceous Period, fights a pack of ferocious *Deinonychus*. This reconstructed scene may well have happened. In the United States, the fossil skeleton of a *Tenontosaurus* was found surrounded by five scattered specimens of *Deinonychus*.

TEETH AND JAWS
Theropods, such as *Megalosaurus*, had long jaws that were usually armed with sharp, serrated teeth. New teeth were ready to replace those that wore out.

Compsognathus
Coelurosaur

Oviraptor
Coelurosaur

Albertosaurus
Carnosaur

TOOLS OF EATING

The coelurosaur *Compsognathus* caught and ate prey with its hands. *Oviraptor* cracked open eggs with its beak. *Albertosaurus* had such short arms it had to tear off chunks of flesh with its powerful jaws. Scientists believe that the fish-eating *Baryonyx*, a theropod dinosaur discovered only in 1983, used the huge, hooklike claw on its hand to spear its prey.

Baryonyx
(not placed in a group)

CUTTERS AND CHOPPERS
The shape of plant-eaters' teeth varied according to their diets. Dinosaurs that ate the hard leaves and fruit of cycads, palms and conifers had thick, peg-shaped teeth. Those that ate the leaves and fruit of softer, flowering plants had thinner, leaf-shaped teeth.

Peg-shaped tooth

Leaf-shaped tooth

Triassic dinosaurs ate horsetail ferns as big as trees.

Jurassic dinosaurs ate pine cones and cycad fruits.

Cretaceous dinosaurs ate flowering plants such as magnolias.

STOMACH STONES
Sauropods, such as *Saltasaurus*, had no grinding teeth. They nipped off leaves with their slender, pencil-like teeth and ground them up with stomach stones called gastroliths. These were ground together by the muscular action of the stomach and crushed tough plant material.

DINOSAUR DINNERS
New varieties of plants evolved on the Earth along with new species of dinosaurs. The plant-eating sauropods, the biggest dinosaurs of all, had to eat huge quantities of plants to provide them with enough energy.

FINGER FOOD
Othnielia, a 1.4-m (5-ft) long gazelle-like dinosaur from the late Jurassic Period, used its five-fingered hands to push aside and hold down a fern while eating it. *Othnielia* had cheek pouches to store food so the tough plant material it ate could be chewed thoroughly later on.

• A PARADE OF DINOSAURS •

Plant-eating Dinosaurs

For most of the dinosaur age, the climate was warm and moist, and plants grew in abundance. Hundreds, perhaps thousands of species of plant-eating dinosaurs browsed on the ferns, cycads and conifers of the Triassic and Jurassic periods, then on the flowering plants of the Cretaceous Period. The bird-hipped ornithopods (the pachycephalosaurs, iguanodonts, duckbills, armoured dinosaurs, and the horned dinosaurs that roamed in huge herds during the late Cretaceous Period) had special cheeks to store plants while they were busy chewing. The lizard-hipped sauropods, which included *Apatosaurus*, *Diplodocus* and *Brachiosaurus*, reached the lush vegetation at the tops of the trees with their long necks. These large plant eaters had large fermenting guts and stomach stones (as shown above) that helped them digest huge amounts of plants.

TEETH AND BEAKS

Palaeontologists can tell much about how a dinosaur lived from the shape of its teeth or its beak, if it had no front teeth. Giraffes' teeth are different from zebras' teeth because giraffes eat tender leaves from the tops of trees, while zebras eat tough, dry grass. In the same way, different families of dinosaurs evolved different kinds of teeth and beaks to cope with a variety of plants.

Protoceratops, one of the smaller horned dinosaurs, had a parrotlike beak for shearing off plant stems, and scissorlike teeth to slice up its food.

Camarasaurus, an 18-m (59-ft) long sauropod, had spoon-shaped cutting teeth but no grinding teeth. However, it could reach high into trees to tear away leaves.

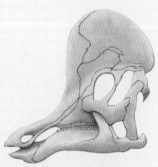

Corythosaurus, a duckbill, tore off leaves with its horny beak, stored them in its cheek pouches, then used rows of strong interlocking teeth to grind them.

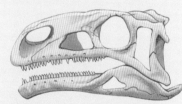

Plateosaurus, an early, long-necked giant, had leaf-shaped teeth to pluck off the leaves of soft plants such as ferns. It did not have grinding teeth.

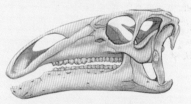

Iguanodon browsed on tough plants such as horsetails, and used its horny beak to nip off leaves. Its rows of ridged, grinding teeth crushed the leaves into a pulp.

STRANGE BUT TRUE

Heterodontosaurus, a plant eater from the early Jurassic Period, had three kinds of teeth. In the front upper jaw it had small cutting teeth; on the lower jaw it had a horny beak. Then it had two pairs of large, fanglike teeth, with grinding teeth at the back.

Long-necked Dinosaurs

LONGEST NECK
Mamenchisaurus had the longest neck of any known animal— an amazing 11 m (36 feet). It could hardly bend its neck, but it could rear up on its hind legs to reach the tops of the highest trees.

The biggest, heaviest and longest land animals that have ever lived were the long-necked sauropod dinosaurs. These strange creatures had long tails, compact bodies, small heads, front legs that were shorter than the hind legs, and clawed first fingers or thumbs that were much larger than their other fingers (they may have used these to hook branches). In 1986, palaeontologists unearthed a few bones from an enormous sauropod named *Seismosaurus* ("earthquake lizard") that may have been more than 30 m (98 ft) long. They have also discovered complete skeletons from sauropods almost as large. *Brachiosaurus*, for example, grew to 23 m (75 ft), stood 12 m (39 ft) high and weighed as much as 12 African elephants. *Brachiosaurus* and the other giants had pillarlike legs to support their great weight, but their skeletons were very light. Their bodies were shaped like giant barrels, and they carried their long tails high off the ground. *Diplodocus'* tail ended in a thin "whiplash"; other sauropods may have had tail clubs for self-defence.

MIGRATING HERDS
Trackways (fossil footprints) and groups of fossils indicate that many sauropods lived in herds and may have migrated to find fresh food, with the adults protecting their young from predators.

Small head
A small head and a small mouth meant *Diplodocus* had to spend a lot of time eating to nourish its huge body.

Strong but light
Struts of bone and air spaces kept *Diplodocus'* skeleton light but strong.

Long legs
With the help of its long front legs, this browser could reach the tender young leaves in the treetops.

LONGER BUT LIGHTER
Diplodocus was longer than *Brachiosaurus*, but weighed only a third as much—partly because the skeleton of *Diplodocus* contained air spaces that reduced its weight but not its strength. The head of a *Diplodocus* was no larger than that of a horse, but its neck was 7 m (23 ft) long and its tail stretched an incredible 14 m (46 feet).

Strong legs
Diplodocus' hind legs were almost solid pillars of bone to support the weight of its intestines and tail muscles.

24

LONGER NECK

Brachiosaurus carried its tiny head high off the ground on the end of a 6-m (20-ft) long neck. Its front legs were almost as long as its hind legs, which gave its already long neck extra reach.

FIT FOR A KING

In 1905, American millionaire Andrew Carnegie presented a plaster cast of *Diplodocus* to the Natural History Museum in London. He had financed the excavation of the original specimen. King Edward VII was there to unwrap the biggest present any king has ever received! Ten copies of the skeleton were sent to other museums around the world.

Whiplash
Diplodocus could injure or stun predators with the bony tip of its 14-m (46-ft) long tail.

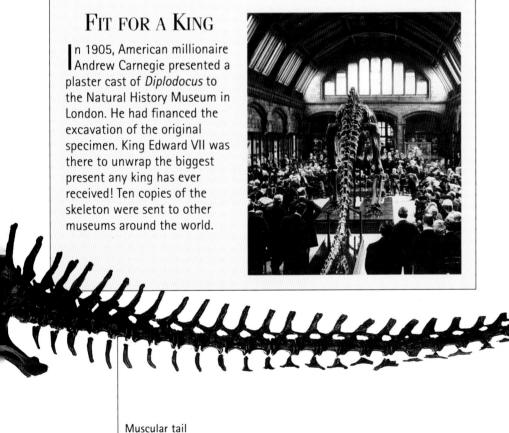

Muscular tail
Diplodocus could not outrun a predator, but its great size and heavy strong tail protected it.

LONG NECK

A modern giraffe, like all mammals, has only seven neck vertebrae. Sauropods, however, had between 12 and 19 neck vertebrae—all with bony struts to provide extra support.

Armoured, Plated and Horned Dinosaurs

Many plant-eating dinosaurs evolved in strange ways to defend themselves against predators or to fight over mates and territories. Pachycephalosaurs, for example, had domed-shaped heads with thick, strong layers of bone. The plated and armoured stegosaurs were slow-moving, small-brained ornithischians that relied on spikes and armour plating to defend themselves. The best known are *Stegosaurus*, a 9-m (30-ft) long, late Jurassic dinosaur that had one or two rows of plates along its back, and two to six pairs of long, sharp spikes at the end of its strong tail; and *Ankylosaurus*, a 10-m (33-ft) long, late Cretaceous dinosaur that was protected by hundreds of bony nodules (some of them with spiky bumps) on its back and sides, and a double-headed club of bone on its tail. The ceratopians, or horned dinosaurs, were the last group of ornithischians to evolve before the dinosaurs died out at the end of the Cretaceous Period. They lived for only 20 million years or so, but spread out across North America and Asia. Ceratopians formed vast herds and used their platelike, horned heads to protect themselves and their young against predators such as *Tyrannosaurus* and *Velociraptor*.

PREDATORS BEWARE!
Styracosaurus, a 5-m (16-ft) long ceratopian, defends its young from a predator by displaying its nose horn and spiked head shield. Its spiky frill protected its neck, and it could use its nose horn to rip open a predator's belly.

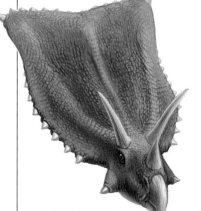

BIG BUT LIGHT
Chasmosaurus' head shield was light and easy to move. It was designed more for display than defence, since this animal could easily outrun predators.

SMALL BUT STRONG
Centrosaurus, a 6-m (20-ft) long ceratopian, was a slow-moving animal that defended itself with its short, heavy head shield.

26

BODY ARMOUR

Kentrosaurus, a 5-m (16-ft) long stegosaur from Africa, had seven pairs of plates from the neck to the middle of the back, and seven pairs of spikes on its back, hips and tail.

SPIKES AND SPINES

Polacanthus, a 4-m (13-ft) long nodosaur, protected its head and vital organs with a double row of vertical spines and used its strong, spiked tail for self-defence.

DISHES AND DAGGERS

Stegosaurus may have used its back plates for defence, or for heating and cooling, but its tail spikes were used for self-defence. They were fused to the bones of the tail, so *Stegosaurus* could swing its spiky tail to scare off a predator.

BUILT FOR DEFENCE

An ankylosaur *Euoplocephalus* from the late Cretaceous Period moved slowly and had a small brain. It could not hope to outwit fast, intelligent predators such as *Velociraptor*. But 6-m (20-ft) long *Euoplocephalus* was very heavily armoured—even its eyelids were protected by bony shutters. It could cause serious damage with the club at the end of its 2.5-m (8-ft) long tail.

A HOLLOW CREST
A male *Parasaurolophus* could stay in touch with other members of the herd or bellow a challenge to another male by forcing air from its mouth up into its hollow crest, then out through its nostrils. It must have had flaps or valves inside the crest to stop it hooting whenever it breathed.

• A PARADE OF DINOSAURS •

Duckbilled Dinosaurs

The duckbilled dinosaurs (hadrosaurs) had broad, ducklike beaks. They walked or ran on their hind legs, and leaned down on their shorter front legs to browse on vegetation. There were many species of duckbills, and they were the most common and widespread plant-eating dinosaurs of the late Cretaceous Period. Hadrosaurs probably evolved in central Asia, but spread to Europe and North America. They had a varied diet, which meant they were able to survive as the Cretaceous climate became drier. All hadrosaurs were closely related, but they looked very different from each other. Some may have had inflatable nose sacs so they could communicate with each other by hooting. Others had hollow crests that acted like echo chambers. They could bellow or call each other by making noises that may have sounded like those made by a modern bassoon (above left).

HEAD OF THE FAMILY

Palaeontologists used to believe that duckbills with different crests belonged to different species. Now they think these different-crested duckbills were members of the same species. A female *Parasaurolophus*, for example, had a medium-sized, curved crest; a young, or juvenile *Parasaurolophus* had a short, fairly straight crest; and an adult male had a long, curved crest. All used their hollow crests to produce sounds that other members of the herd would understand.

Adult female

Adult male

Juvenile

A DUCK'S BILL
Like all hadrosaurs, 13-m (43-ft) long *Edmontosaurus* had a toothless duckbill, covered with leathery skin, which it used to pluck leaves and fruits. It had batteries of teeth in the back of its mouth and it chewed food by moving its jaw up and down so the overlapping teeth crushed its food.

CHOPPING AND GRINDING
Seen close up, *Edmontosaurus'* tooth batteries consisted of scores of tiny, leaf-shaped teeth, which acted like a cheese grater.

DID YOU KNOW?
Saurolophus, which had only a small, hornlike crest, may have produced noises by inflating a skin-covered sac on top of its nose. This would have been supported by the crest at the back of its head.

LIVING TOGETHER
Like giraffes (which eat tree leaves) and zebras (which eat low-growing plants), flat-headed and crested duckbills were able to live together without taking one another's food supply.

Discover more in The Cretaceous World

29

Record-breaking Dinosaurs

The dinosaurs were one of the world's most successful group of animals. They were the biggest, heaviest and longest land animals that have ever lived, and they dominated the Earth for 150 million years. Compared to this record, the five million years that humans have been on Earth seems like the blink of an eye. Dinosaurs were the world's strangest and most extraordinary animals. It has always been hard for people to imagine a world populated by such huge creatures: the remains of the first dinosaur ever described, 9-m (30-ft) long *Megalosaurus*, were first thought to belong to a human giant. It has also been hard for people to understand just how spectacular the dinosaurs were. *Seismosaurus*, the "earthquake lizard" and the biggest of the sauropods, may have been more than 30 m (98 ft) long. Only a few of its bones have ever been found: a 2.4-m (8-ft) long shoulder blade, taller than the biggest human giant; and a 1.5-m (5-ft) long vertebra. The ground must have quaked with each footstep from this gigantic creature.

SMALLEST
Compsognathus was one of the smallest known dinosaurs. It was only 1 m (3 ft) long, weighed just 3.5 kg (8 lb), and stood no taller than a chicken. It must have been a swift and efficient hunter. One specimen was found with the bones of a tiny lizard in its stomach cavity.

HEAVIEST
Weighing 80 tonnes (78 tons), 23-m (75-ft) long *Brachiosaurus* was as tall as a four-storey building. Its shoulders were more than 6 m (20 ft) off the ground and its humerus, or upper arm bone, was 2 m (7 ft) long. The humerus of an adult human is only about 35 cm (1 ft) long.

DID YOU KNOW?
What do a *Struthiomimus* (whose name means "ostrich-mimic") and an ostrich have in common? They can both sprint swiftly on very long slim legs (an ostrich can outrun a horse) and have long thin necks with small heads.

FASTEST
Struthiomimus, stood 2 m (7 ft) high and was 3–4 m (10–13 ft) long. It defended itself against predators by running at speeds of up to 50 km (31 miles) per hour, balancing on its long, birdlike hind legs.

LONGEST NECK

Mamenchisaurus, at 22 m (72 ft), was almost as long as its close relative *Diplodocus*, but it had a fairly short tail. Its 11-m (36-ft) long neck, which it used to reach the tops of tall trees, is the longest neck of any known animal.

LONGEST

With more than half of its total length of 23 m (75 ft) taken up by its 14-m (46-ft) long tail, *Diplodocus* was the longest known dinosaur. It would have used its strong, whiplash tail to defend itself against predators such as *Allosaurus*.

BIGGEST PREDATOR

Tyrannosaurus was bigger than any predator except the sperm whale. It could grow up to 14 m (46 ft) long and was taller than a double-decker bus. It weighed 7 tonnes (7 tons).

BIG, BIGGER, BIGGEST

In the 1970s and 1980s, fossil hunters found massive bones from sauropods even bigger than 23-m (75-ft) long *Brachiosaurus*. Called *Supersaurus, Ultrasaurus,* and *Seismosaurus*, these incredible animals may have been 30 m (98 ft) long! In this photograph, palaeontologist Dr James Jensen stands next to the reconstructed front leg of one of these giants. These fossils are still being unearthed, and it may take 10–20 years to reconstruct their skeletons. Then they will topple the record-breakers of today.

MOST TEETH

Anatotitan, a duckbilled dinosaur, had about 1,000 tiny, leaf-shaped teeth arranged in rows of 200–250 on each side of its upper and lower jaws, all at the back of its mouth. Two mummified fossils of this species have been found, complete with the remains of their last meals: pine needles, twigs, seeds and fruits.

Fossilised Clues

We rely on fossils for clues about how dinosaurs lived. But dinosaur fossils are very rare. The chances of a plant or animal becoming fossilised were low because conditions had to be just right for fossilisation to occur. An animal had to be fairly big (small dinosaurs had delicate bones that were easily scattered or destroyed, or eaten by scavengers), and it had to die in the right place. If a dinosaur's body was washed into a lake, for example, silt would cover it up quite quickly and its bones were more likely to be preserved. In most cases only the bones of the dinosaurs were preserved (a few turned into minerals such as opal), but occasionally the animal was covered by sand or volcanic ash that preserved or mummified the body and left an impression of the texture of its skin. Sometimes only a dinosaur's footprints or its droppings have been preserved. Palaeontologists use all these clues to piece together pictures of the creatures that lived so many millions of years ago.

BACK IN TIME
The deeper a layer of rock, the older it is. The oldest and deepest rocks contain single-celled bacteria and algae. More complex plants and animals are found in the newer rocks above.

A FOSSIL IN THE MAKING
A 6-m (20-ft) long *Camptosaurus* lies at the water's edge, dead of disease or old age. The hot sun has begun to dry the body, and if scavengers do not tear it apart, it will be covered by silt and gradually fossilised. The *Coelurus* shown here are eating the insects and other animals around the carcass. Their jaws are too weak for the thick skin of *Camptosaurus*.

MONGOLIAN FOSSIL SITES

Mongolia, in central Asia, is covered by sand and desert today. During the Jurassic and early Cretaceous periods, Mongolia was warm and moist, with lakes and shallow seas. Many species of dinosaur lived in this ideal environment.

NORTH AMERICAN FOSSIL SITES

North America was warm and moist in the Jurassic and early Cretaceous periods. Great herds of plant eaters lived there, but they disappeared when the climate became colder and more changeable towards the end of the Cretaceous Period.

BONES THAT ARE NOT BONES

Skeletons can fossilise in different ways. In a petrified fossil (right), preserved bones that form partial or complete skeletons have outer and middle layers that have been replaced by minerals. They literally "turn to stone". A cast is formed when mud fills the hollow spaces inside bones—this occasionally happens with a dinosaur's brain or the canals of its middle ear. The bone then rots away. Sometimes fossil skulls are hollow, and scientists can make a mould of the dinosaur's brain. Very rarely, a dinosaur is mummified in dry sand that gradually hardens into rock, leaving an impression of the animal's skin.

OUT OF REACH
Beneath the surface of a lake, a dead dinosaur is safe from large scavengers. Its flesh rots away or is eaten by fish and the skeleton remains intact.

COVER-UP
Layers of sand or silt cover the dinosaur's bones, and stop them from being washed away.

FOSSILISATION
Trapped and flattened by layers of sediment, the dinosaur's bones are gradually replaced by minerals that are harder than the rocks around them.

FOSSIL FINDS
Millions of years later, upheavals in the Earth's crust bring the dinosaur's fossilised skeleton close to the surface, where it is exposed by the weather and erosion.

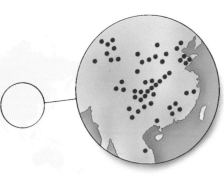

Discover more in Skeletons and Skulls

Skeletons and Skulls

Most of the dinosaurs we know about were much bigger than even large modern mammals. An average-sized dinosaur such as *Camptosaurus* was about 6.5 m (21 ft) long—a third longer than an African elephant. But *Camptosaurus* weighed only about 3 tonnes (3 tons)—less than half the weight of an elephant. Dinosaurs had two distinct body types: a bipedal fast-running kind such as *Hypsilophodon,* and a quadrupedal heavy type such as *Camarasaurus.* They could grow to enormous sizes because their skeletons were superbly engineered; they were very strong without being very heavy. The vertebrae of the giant sauropods were supported by struts and thin sheets of bone because they were almost hollow; solid vertebrae would have made these animals too heavy to stand upright. Most dinosaurs had holes in their skulls. Meat eaters had the largest holes of all to accommodate the bulging and powerful jaw muscles that opened and closed their jaws.

Skull
This 1.5-m (5-ft) long, lightly built "gazelle" of the dinosaur world had a horny beak at the front of its mouth, a fairly large brain and large openings for the eyes.

Backbone
Extra ribs in front of the shoulders supported the neck muscles.

HYPSILOPHODON

Hands
Four long clawed fingers were used to grasp plant food or to support *Hypsilophodon* as it grazed on low-growing plants.

CAMARASAURUS

Backbone
Like the steel rods of a crane, the vertebrae provided support where it was needed most.

Skull
This 18-m (59-ft) long sauropod had a small head. The large openings on top of the skull may have helped to cool the small brain.

Leg bones
Like all sauropods, *Camarasaurus* had massive, pillarlike legs to carry its great weight.

Chest
Very deep ribs supported the large stomach *Camarasaurus* needed to digest its tough plant food.

Hind feet
Camarasaurus's toes could spread out for support as it reared up to reach young leaves in the treetops.

Front feet
Five strong clawed toes helped to support the weight of the chest, neck and head.

CERATOSAURUS

This 6-m (20-ft) long predator had a strong lower jaw and a high, narrow skull. Both had large cavities to make space for the huge jaw muscles that drove razor-sharp fangs.

OURANOSAURUS

Although its jaw muscles were weak, *Ouranosaurus* was an efficient plant feeder. As it closed its mouth, the bones of the upper jaw moved apart, breaking up food with bands of cheek teeth.

DINOSAUR BRAINS

Dinosaurs had small brains, but this does not mean they were stupid. Brain size is not the most important factor. Brain complexity and brain size in relation to total body size are far more important. *Iguanodon's* body was as big as a bus; its brain was no bigger than a goose's egg. *Iguanodon* did not need much intelligence to find its food of leaves and fruit. *Deinonychus*, however, had to see, smell and chase fast-running animals. Its brain was the size of an apple, even though its body was smaller than a car. But the "thinking" part of a dinosaur's brain, the cerebrum, was much smaller than a mammal's cerebrum, which meant that a dinosaur could not have learned new things as easily as a monkey or a dog could today.

Rhesus monkey

Iguanodon

Tail

Spines on the undersides of the tail vertebrae supported muscles that helped *Hypsilophodon* carry its tail off the ground.

Leg bones

Hypsilophodon was a fast runner. As its femur was very short, the long tibia and foot could swing forward to give the dinosaur great speed.

Feet

Long, strong toes like those of an ostrich gave *Hypsilophodon* a sure footing as it sprinted away from danger.

DID YOU KNOW?

Stegosaurus's brain was the size of a walnut. A cavity in the vertebrae above its hips may have housed a gland that produced energy-rich glycogen. This gave *Stegosaurus* a burst of speed if it needed to escape from a predator.

IN THE NOSE

Corythosaurus (left) may have drawn air in through the nostrils at the front of its snout and into its hollow crest to produce sounds. *Brachiosaurus* had nostrils on the top of its head, possibly to help keep its body cool.

BUILT FOR STRENGTH

The tibia and femur of *Tyrannosaurus* were the same length, and had powerful muscles attached to them. *Tyrannosaurus* could charge at its prey with a sudden burst of energy, but its legs were not designed for a long chase.

Discover more in Plant-eating Dinosaurs

Footprints and Other Clues

ARMOUR PLATING
Dinosaur skin, like that of living reptiles, was made up of scales, sometimes with bony lumps (called osteoderms), that provided protection against predators' teeth.

Fossilised teeth and bones tell us much about how dinosaurs looked and lived. But palaeontologists also use other clues to piece together pictures of the dinosaurs' day-to-day lives. Skin impressions show that dinosaurs were protected against predators and spiky plants by a tough covering of skin. Fossil footprints, called trackways, tell us how dinosaurs moved about, and that sauropods, hadrosaurs and horned dinosaurs travelled in herds. The remains of nests show that dinosaurs built nests close to each other for protection against predators and scavengers. The fossils of eggs and even baby dinosaurs indicate how small these animals were when they hatched and how quickly they grew. The bones of adult dinosaurs give clues to their diet, injuries and the cause of their death, while fossilised dung provides information about what dinosaurs ate.

TRACKING FOSSIL FOOTPRINTS
Footprints show that many dinosaurs travelled in groups. These *Apatosaurus* prints were made by five adults moving in the same direction.

DAILY DIET
Coprolites (fossilised dung) have been found containing hard seeds, pieces of pine cones, and even plant stems.

STORIES IN STONE
Small plant eaters stick close to a herd of long-necked sauropods as it migrates across the late Jurassic landscape of North America. Sharp-clawed theropods shadow the herd, hoping to pick off a sick or injured animal.

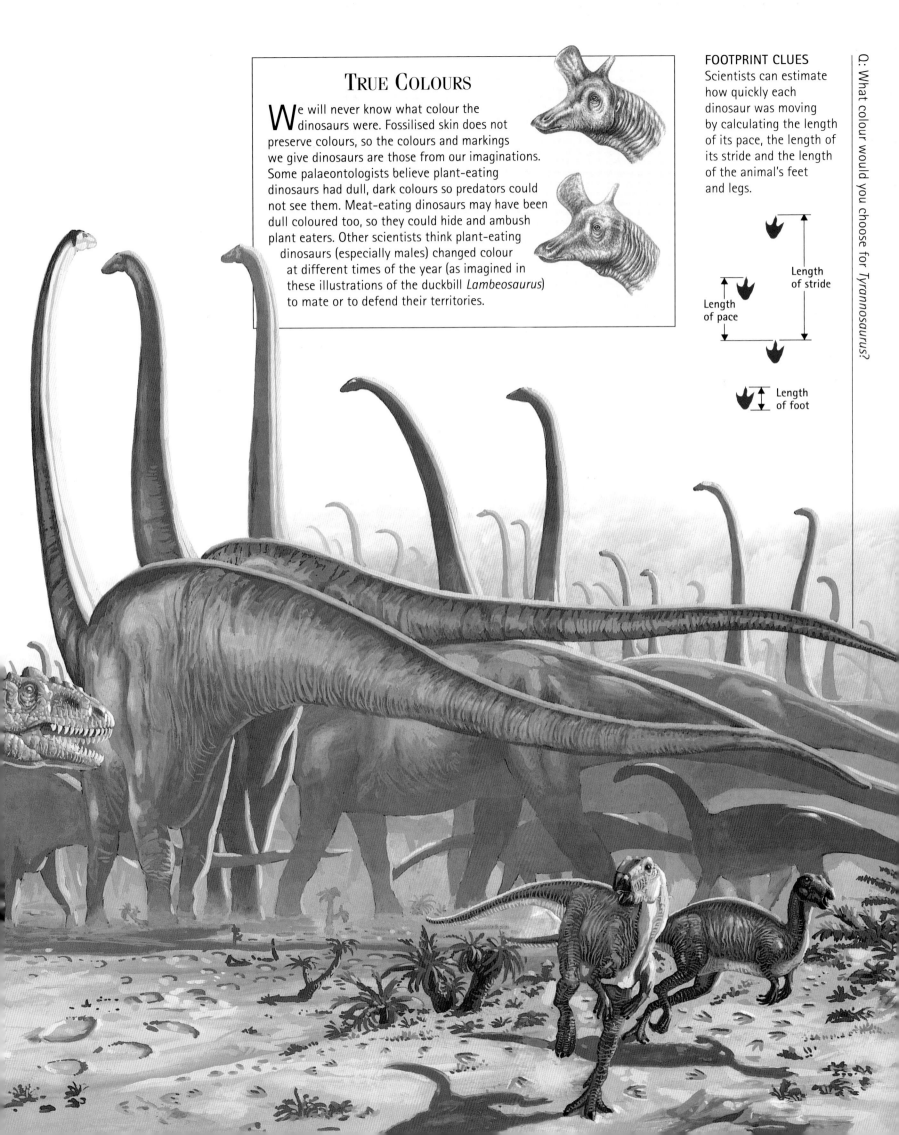

True Colours

We will never know what colour the dinosaurs were. Fossilised skin does not preserve colours, so the colours and markings we give dinosaurs are those from our imaginations. Some palaeontologists believe plant-eating dinosaurs had dull, dark colours so predators could not see them. Meat-eating dinosaurs may have been dull coloured too, so they could hide and ambush plant eaters. Other scientists think plant-eating dinosaurs (especially males) changed colour at different times of the year (as imagined in these illustrations of the duckbill *Lambeosaurus*) to mate or to defend their territories.

FOOTPRINT CLUES
Scientists can estimate how quickly each dinosaur was moving by calculating the length of its pace, the length of its stride and the length of the animal's feet and legs.

Length of stride

Length of pace

Length of foot

Q: What colour would you choose for *Tyrannosaurus*?

ON GUARD

The *Maiasaura* nests discovered by Dr Horner were spaced about 7 m (23 ft) apart, the same length as an average adult, so *Maiasaura* had enough space to avoid accidentally crushing one another's eggs. However, they were close enough to protect the nests from possible egg thieves such as *Oviraptor*.

Amniotic sac
A fluid-filled bag cushioned the embryo.

Chorion
This membrane provided oxygen.

Yolk sac
This provided nourishment.

Eggshell
Dinosaur young developed inside a sealed container.

A DINOSAUR NURSERY

Up to 25 eggs were laid in each *Maiasaura* nest, which was a 2-m (7-ft) wide, 1-m (3-ft) deep bowl scooped out of mud. The hatchlings were about 50 cm (1½ ft) long.

• LIFE AS A DINOSAUR •

Raising a Family

Palaeontologists used to think that dinosaurs did not look after their eggs or their young because very few dinosaur nests had been discovered. In 1978, however, Dr John Horner found a duckbill dinosaur nesting site in North America, with dozens of nests spaced just far enough apart so that adult dinosaurs could guard their own eggs without stepping on another dinosaur's nest. He also found fossil eggshells and the fossils of 15 baby duckbills. The babies had already grown much larger than when they were born, but they had not left the nest because they were still being cared for by their parents. Dr Horner called these dinosaurs *Maiasaura*, or "good mother lizards".

Palaeontologists know that at least two meat eaters, *Troodon* and *Oviraptor*, laid eggs. Fossil eggs from the giant sauropods have been found in Europe, South America and China, but we do not know how these enormous creatures managed to lay their eggs safely.

Chicken's egg

Possible
theropod egg

Oviraptor's egg

Emu's egg

BIG BODIES, SMALL EGGS

Dinosaur eggs were very small in proportion to their bodies. Very large eggs would have very thick shells, and these could never be broken by the hatchlings.

A Terrible Egg Thief?

Many palaeontologists believe that *Oviraptor*, a theropod from the late Cretaceous Period, stole eggs from the nests of other dinosaurs. Its strong jaws could have easily broken eggshells and crushed the bones of the young dinosaurs it caught with its clawed hands. The first *Oviraptor* fossil, discovered in Mongolia in 1924 with a clutch of eggs, seemed to confirm this belief. Palaeontologists thought the eggs belonged to a *Protoceratops*, but new evidence has shown that the eggs did in fact belong to *Oviraptor*. The debate continues.

Did You Know?

Microscopic examination of *Maiasaura* embryos and hatchlings shows that they had very poorly developed joints in their legs. They had to be cared for by their parents. Hypsilophodons (the cousins of hadrosaurs such as *Maiasaura*), however, had strong legs and could fend for themselves as soon as they hatched.

Discover more in Duckbilled Dinosaurs

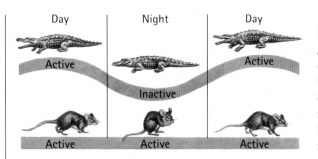

Day	Night	Day
Active	Inactive	Active
Active	Active	Active

UPS AND DOWNS
A cold-blooded reptile, such as a crocodile, must bask in the sunlight before it is warm enough to move quickly. But a warm-blooded mammal, such as a mouse, can be active all the time. Its body temperature stays the same no matter how cold it is outside.

Staying cool
Spongy skin over the sail would have allowed heat to radiate quickly. Even a small drop in the temperature of the blood would have helped *Ouranosaurus* to stay cool.

Cooling the blood
A complex system of small veins carried warm blood up into *Ouranosaurus'* sail, where it was cooled before it flowed back down into the body.

Keeping Warm; Keeping Cool

Every animal needs to keep its body temperature stable. If it cannot stay warm, it will not have enough energy to move about. If it becomes too warm, its brain may overheat and its breathing and digestion will not work properly. Dinosaurs had different ways to keep their bodies at stable temperatures. Some had frills, plates, sails or spikes to help them warm or cool their blood. Some scientists believe that dinosaurs may have had divided hearts to pump blood into their brains. This advanced body structure would probably have included an internal temperature control, or warm-bloodedness. The small, energetic meat eaters may have been warm-blooded, but this does not seem to be true for large, adult dinosaurs. Their bodies had a wide surface area, which meant they were able to radiate heat quickly and maintain a stable temperature.

AIR CONDITIONING
Ouranosaurus could warm up quickly in the morning, then cool down by the afternoon by pumping blood under the skin of the spiny "sail" on its back.

HOT PLATES

Tuojiangosaurus had 15 pairs of bony plates along its back. Some palaeontologists think the plates were covered by skin that was rich with blood to help the dinosaur warm up or cool down quickly.

BIVALVES

A divided heart separates blood that flows under high pressure to the body from blood that flows under low pressure to and from the lungs. Some scientists think that tall or fast-moving two-legged dinosaurs needed a high-pressure blood supply to their brains and muscles.

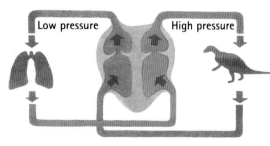

Low pressure   High pressure

NECKS AND TAILS

Sauropods had long necks to help them reach the treetops, and long tails to balance their long necks. Their necks and tails provided a large surface area to soak up heat from the sun or to cool them down in the middle of the day.

A CHANGE IN TEMPERATURE

Scientists have looked at dinosaur bones under a microscope, and believe these reptiles may have been both warm-blooded and cold-blooded. Dinosaurs seem to have grown quickly (like warm-blooded mammals) when they were young, then more slowly (like cold-blooded reptiles) when they became adults. But small meat eaters, such as *Dromiceiomimus* (left), were very active predators, hunting lizards and insects. They would have needed a constantly stable temperature and may have been more warm-blooded as adults than other dinosaurs.

Nostril

STRANGE BUT TRUE

Sauropods such as *Brachiosaurus* could "let off steam" when they became too hot by pumping blood through the delicate skin inside their huge nostrils. This cooled the blood so the rest of the body could then keep cool.

Discover more in What is a dinosaur?

41

A WIDE VARIETY
Like a duckbilled dinosaur, this rhinoceros has a wide mouth so it can eat many types of plants.

SPECIAL DIETS
Like a horned dinosaur, this gazelle chooses its food carefully, plucking leaves and fruit with its narrow mouth.

Into the mouth
Palaeontologists do not know if *Apatosaurus* had a muscular tongue or used its peglike teeth to rake leaves or twigs into its mouth.

Down the neck
Powerful muscles pushed food down *Apatosaurus'* 6-m (20-ft) long oesophagus, a tube running from the mouth to the stomach.

Living reptile
Crocodile teeth are designed to grip, not cut.

Large theropod
Tyrannosaurus tooth

Eating and Digesting

Different dinosaurs ate and digested their food in various ways. Scientists have learnt about these dietary habits by studying dinosaur teeth and bones, analysing dinosaur dung and observing how living animals eat and digest their food. Palaeontologists have found fossils of dinosaurs that sliced and ripped meat, dinosaurs that chewed plants or ground leaves into a paste before swallowing them, and toothless dinosaurs that ate eggs. The meat eaters had sharp teeth to cut up meat, which is easier to digest than coarse plants. *Tyrannosaurus'* sharp, serrated teeth were designed so that its prey's struggles actually helped it tear off chunks of flesh. Large plant-eating dinosaurs had internal features such as stomach stones (gastroliths) to help grind and digest the large quantity of plants they ate.

Small theropod
Troodon tooth

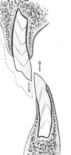

Upper jaw

Lower jaw

CUTTING DOWN TO SIZE
Styracosaurus used rows of scissorlike teeth to snip leaves into small pieces.

GRINDING TO A PASTE
Edmontosaurus used batteries of grinding teeth to crush leaves into a paste.

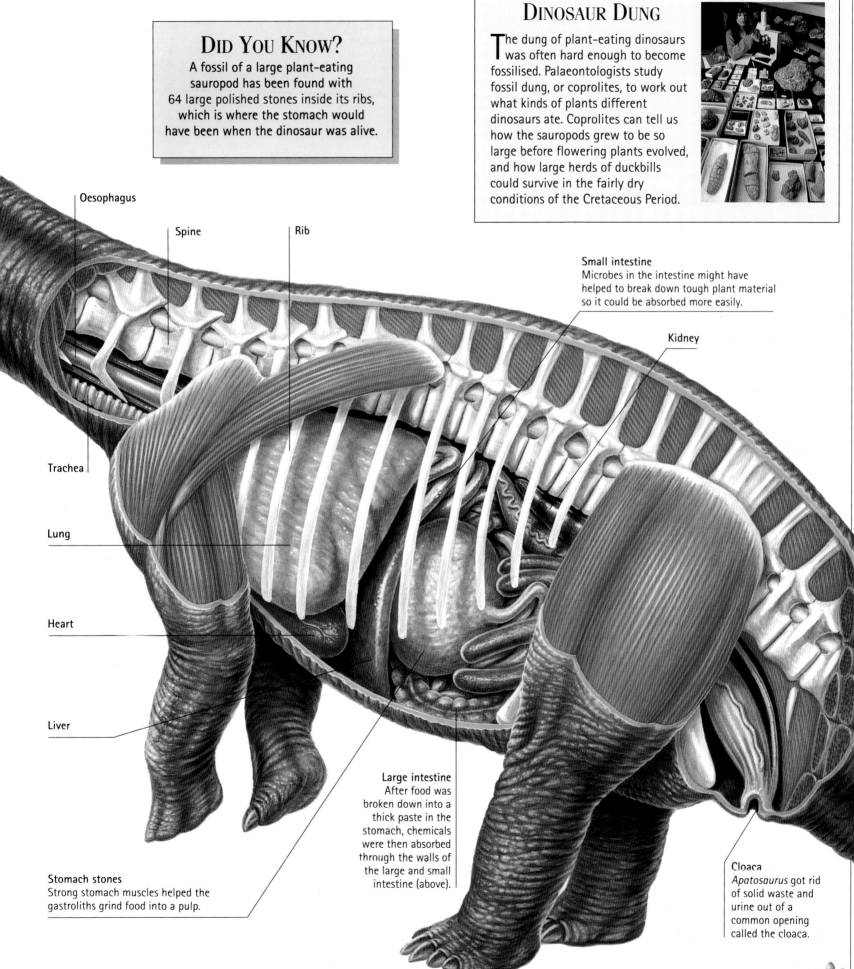

DID YOU KNOW?

A fossil of a large plant-eating sauropod has been found with 64 large polished stones inside its ribs, which is where the stomach would have been when the dinosaur was alive.

DINOSAUR DUNG

The dung of plant-eating dinosaurs was often hard enough to become fossilised. Palaeontologists study fossil dung, or coprolites, to work out what kinds of plants different dinosaurs ate. Coprolites can tell us how the sauropods grew to be so large before flowering plants evolved, and how large herds of duckbills could survive in the fairly dry conditions of the Cretaceous Period.

Oesophagus

Spine

Rib

Small intestine
Microbes in the intestine might have helped to break down tough plant material so it could be absorbed more easily.

Kidney

Trachea

Lung

Heart

Liver

Large intestine
After food was broken down into a thick paste in the stomach, chemicals were then absorbed through the walls of the large and small intestine (above).

Stomach stones
Strong stomach muscles helped the gastroliths grind food into a pulp.

Cloaca
Apatosaurus got rid of solid waste and urine out of a common opening called the cloaca.

Discover more in Footprints and Other Clues

43

A SPIKY SHIELD

Triceratops' neck was a massive frill of solid bone with 1-m (3-ft) long horns that protected its neck and chest from an attack by another *Triceratops* or a predator.

BUILT LIKE A TANK

Euoplocephalus was protected by bands of armour, bony studs on the shoulders and a heavy, bony skull. It could injure a predator by lashing out with a bony club at the end of its tail.

STABBING TAIL

To defend itself against a predator, *Tuojiangosaurus* used its muscular tail, which was armed at the tip with two pairs of sharp spikes.

MULTI-PURPOSE TAIL

Diplodocus' tail was longer than a tennis court. It used the tail for support when it reared up to crush a predator with its front legs or swung it like a whip to blind or stun an attacker.

• LIFE AS A DINOSAUR •

Attack and Defence

Many dinosaurs used their horns, spikes or armour to defend themselves. But even those without armour had their own defence weapons. *Apatosaurus* could rear up on its hind legs and crush an attacker with its front feet, or use its tail to injure a predator. Many sauropods travelled in herds, relying on safety in numbers so that only weak or sick animals would be attacked. The bird-mimic dinosaurs such as *Gallimimus* used their speed to escape, while *Pachycephalosaurus* could use its thick skull to defend itself against predators and other members of its own species. Meat eaters had speed, agility and sharp teeth for effective attack and defence. Large predators such as *Tyrannosaurus* hunted alone, and relied on a surprise rush. We will never know if dinosaurs used camouflage. Perhaps some species of plant eaters had dappled skin so they could hide from predators. Meat eaters may have used the same kind of disguise to ambush their prey.

THE TERRIBLE CLAW

Just as a falcon uses its razor-sharp claws to kill its prey, *Deinonychus* (whose name means "terrible claw") used the 13-cm (5-in), swivel claw on the second toe of each foot to kill its prey. It would leap into the air to kick or balance on one leg as it slashed at the skin of plant eaters. Fossils of five *Deinonychus* have been found beside the body of a *Tenontosaurus*, which suggests that the fast-moving, big-brained *Deinonychus* hunted in packs.

BATTERING RAM
Pachycephalosaurus' skeleton was designed to withstand its charging attacks against other males, or predators.

HEAD TO HEAD
Two 4.5-m (15-ft) long male *Pachycephalosaurus* are butting heads like mountain goats to see which will mate with a herd of females. Although protected by a solid dome of bone 25 cm (10 in) thick, one has become dizzy and is about to plummet to its death.

BIG BANG
According to one theory, several volcanic eruptions produced climatic changes that wiped out the dinosaurs.

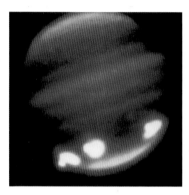

METEORITE HITS
Perhaps a giant meteorite hit the Earth, causing dust clouds, acid rain, storms and huge waves.

END OF AN ERA
When the dinosaurs died out, all large land animals disappeared. Late Cretaceous mammals were small (*Alphadon*, shown here, was only 30 cm [1 ft] long) but evolved rapidly into thousands of new species to replace the dinosaurs.

Why did they vanish?

The extinction of the dinosaurs 65 million years ago was the most mysterious and dramatic disappearance of a group of animals in the history of the Earth. But the dinosaurs were not the only animals to die out. More than half of the world's animals also disappeared, including the pterosaurs and large marine reptiles. The number of species of dinosaurs had been dropping for at least eight million years, but some species were common right up to the "K/T boundary", which marks the end of the Cretaceous Period and the beginning of the Tertiary Period. Some scientists believe that a volcanic disaster or a giant meteorite wiped out the dinosaurs. Others argue that such a disaster—causing disease, rising sea levels and gradual changes in climate—would have affected all animal life. Another theory combines these thoughts: changes in weather and sea levels had already reduced the amount of land and food for dinosaurs, and they were unable to cope with a sudden disaster.

INTO THE FUTURE
Even today, habitat loss through earthquakes, storms or human activity such as clearing forests, is threatening the future of many animals.

STRANGE BUT TRUE
People have produced some weird and wonderful theories to explain why the dinosaurs disappeared. Some suggest they died of boredom, "drowned" in their own droppings, were hunted by aliens, or even committed suicide!

VICTIMS AND SURVIVORS
None of the current theories can explain why some animal groups disappeared, while others survived. Pterosaurs died out, but birds did not. Dinosaurs vanished, but small land reptiles and mammals survived. Mosasaurs, plesiosaurs and pliosaurs were wiped out, but turtles and crocodiles are still alive today.

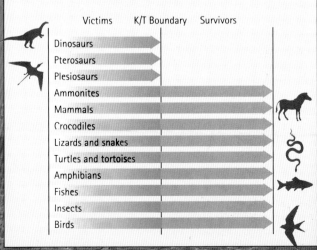

Victims	K/T Boundary	Survivors
Dinosaurs		
Pterosaurs		
Plesiosaurs		
Ammonites		
Mammals		
Crocodiles		
Lizards and snakes		
Turtles and tortoises		
Amphibians		
Fishes		
Insects		
Birds		

Surviving Relatives

FEATHER FOSSILS
The detailed impressions of feathers on this *Archaeopteryx* fossil confirm an important evolutionary link between reptiles and birds.

SCALY SURVIVORS
Crocodilians have hardly changed since the beginning of the Cretaceous Period. They have evolved slowly because they live in a stable environment.

D inosaurs are dead, but it seems that certain dinosaur features live on in other animals. Dinosaurs and birds, for example, are very different animals but they have many characteristics in common. Scientists are now convinced that dinosaurs were the ancestors of birds. The skeleton of *Archaeopteryx*, the earliest known bird, was very similar to that of the lizard-hipped carnivorous dinosaur *Compsognathus*. Many scientists now classify *Archaeopteryx* as a small, flesh-eating dinosaur with feathers (fossilised feather shown left). Dinosaurs are also related to crocodilians, which survived the great extinction at the end of the Cretaceous Period. Crocodilians and dinosaurs have very similar skulls and common ancestors—the archosaurs. The dinosaurs disappeared, but crocodilians today are almost the same as their ancestors. Their way of life has changed little in 150 million years.

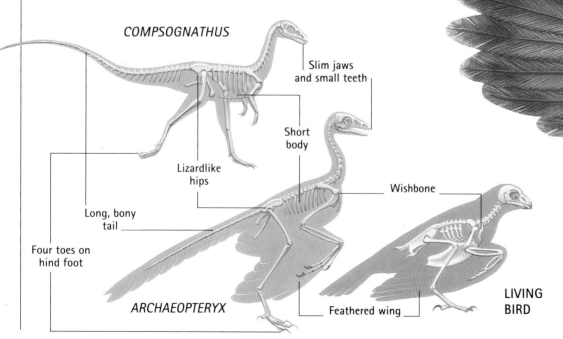

COMPSOGNATHUS

Slim jaws and small teeth

Short body

Lizardlike hips

Wishbone

Long, bony tail

Four toes on hind foot

ARCHAEOPTERYX

Feathered wing

LIVING BIRD

FROM DINOSAUR TO BIRD
Fossil records show a strong similarity between small carnivorous dinosaurs that ran upright on long, slim hind legs, *Archaeopteryx*, and living birds.

FLIGHT PATH

Archaeopteryx could fly by flapping its broad wings but more often it would dive from its perch onto prey such as insects and small reptiles.

FAMILY TREE

Alligators and crocodiles

Ornithischian dinosaurs

Saurischian dinosaurs

Birds

Ornithosuchus

TRIASSIC	JURASSIC	CRETACEOUS	TERTIARY	QUATERNARY

RESEMBLING THE PAST

Some of today's birds are very similar to dinosaurs in their structure and behaviour. The secretary bird of Africa rarely flies, but runs after insects, small reptiles and mammals on its hind legs—just as the dinosaur *Compsognathus* did. Baby hoatzins, from South America, use claws on the front of their wings to climb about in trees—just as *Archaeopteryx* did.

Hoatzin

Secretary bird

INGENIOUS BUT INACCURATE
In 1853, an *Iguanodon* was constructed in the Crystal Palace in London. It looked just like a giant, prehistoric iguana.

REPTILIAN HUMANS
If dinosaurs had not become extinct, would some have evolved to resemble humans?

• THE END OF THE DINOSAURS •

Myths and Tall Tales

Dinosaurs have been the subjects of myths and tall tales for years. When people first began to discover dinosaur fossils, they had many imaginative theories about the creatures that had such enormous bones. The earliest description of a dinosaur fossil came from China, almost 3,000 years ago. Chinese scholars thought the fossils were dragon bones. More than 300 years ago, a *Megalosaurus*' thigh bone dug up in England was believed to be the bone of an elephant, then a giant human. In 1820, a scientist thought that dinosaur trackways had been made by prehistoric giant birds. Dinosaurs died out 61 million years before humans appeared, but movies have shown them attacking people who lived in caves. In the past 50 years, however, we have begun to dispel many of the misunderstandings about these amazing animals.

50

DRAGONS AND DINOSAURS

When Chinese scholars found dinosaur fossils they imagined they belonged to great and powerful dragons, thought to bring good fortune to their people.

DID YOU KNOW?

The ancient Chinese ground up dinosaur fossils to make powerful medicines and special magic powders. Even today, tiny amounts of these powdered "dragon bones" are used in some traditional Chinese medicines.

CREEPING DINOSAURS

Early scientists could not believe that dinosaurs walked upright on straight legs. They thought these strange reptiles crept on sprawled legs.

A STONE-AGE MYTH

Television has helped to keep myths alive by showing humans flying on pterosaurs, working with dinosaurs and even keeping them as pets.

A DINOSAUR REVIVAL

People are understandably fascinated by dinosaurs. These diverse creatures ruled the world for 150 million years, and were able to meet the challenges of a changing planet. Now, dinosaurs have "reappeared" in modern life. The box-office hit *Jurassic Park* stars a whole cast of plant- and meat-eating dinosaurs. A brightly painted reconstruction of *Allosaurus* (right) might be seen on the back of a car. You can also buy dinosaur balloons, cartoons, posters, stickers and books.

Discover more in Why did they vanish?

Allosaurus
Al-oh-sore-us:
"Different reptile"
Group: meat eater
Period: late Jurassic–early
Cretaceous
Discovered: North America, 1877
Size: up to 12 m (39 ft)

Plateosaurus
Plat-ee-oh-sore-us:
"Flat reptile"
Group: plant eater
Period: late Triassic
Discovered: Europe, 1837
Size: 8 m (26 ft) long

Coelophysis
Seel-oh-fie-sis:
"Hollow shape"
Group: meat eater
Period: late Triassic
Discovered: North
America, 1889
Size: 3 m (10 ft) long

Coelurus
Seel-ure-us:
"Hollow tail"
Group: meat eater
Period: late Jurassic
Discovered: North America,
1879
Size: 2 m (7 ft) long

Euoplocephalus
You-op-loh-keff-a-lus:
"True plated head"
Group: plant eater
Period: late Cretaceous
Discovered: North America, 1910
Size: 6 m (20 ft) long

Stegosaurus
Steg-oh-sore-us:
"Roof lizard"
Group: meat eater
Period: late Jurassic
Discovered: United States,
1877
Size: up to 9 m (30 ft)

Saltasaurus
Salt-a-sore-us:
"Salt reptile"
Group: plant eater
Period: late Cretaceous
Discovered: South
America, 1970
Size: 12 m (39 ft) long

• THE END OF THE DINOSAURS •

Identification Parade

Dinosaurs marched across 150 million years, and represented an amazingly successful and varied group of land animals. They prospered for many times longer than human beings have done. Although we will never know exactly how many kinds of dinosaurs there were, we know enough about their evolution to see their steady progress from only a few species during the Triassic Period to almost twice as many during the Jurassic Period. This was followed by an incredible "flowering" during the Cretaceous Period, when there were more species of dinosaurs than during both preceding periods. Dinosaurs have taught us many valuable lessons about evolution, and about how groups of animals spread across the land, dominating the world before they disappeared. But we are left with only tantalising clues about how dinosaurs lived.

Pachycephalosaurus
Pack-ee-keff-ah-low-sore-us:
"Thick-headed reptile"
Group: plant eater
Period: late Cretaceous
Discovered: North America, 1943
Size: 8 m (26 ft) long

Maiasaura
My-ah-sore-ah:
"Good mother lizard"
Group: plant eater
Period: late Cretaceous
Discovered: North America, 1979
Size: up to 9 m (30 ft)

Brachiosaurus
Brak-ee-oh-sore-us:
"Arm reptile"
Group: plant eater
Period: late Jurassic
Discovered: North America, 1903
Size: up to 23 m (75 ft)

Deinonychus
Die-non-i-kus:
"Terrible claw"
Group: meat eater
Period: early Cretaceous
Discovered: North
  America, 1969
Size: 3 m (10 ft) long

Hypsilophodon
Hip-sih-loh-foe-don:
"High-ridged tooth"
Group: plant eater
Period: early Cretaceous
Discovered: Europe, 1870
Size: 2 m (7 ft) long

DINOSAURS TODAY

When Richard Owen invented the name dinosaur 150 years ago, we knew of just nine species. Today we know of at least 1,000, which includes an incredible variety of plant eaters, meat eaters and egg thieves, dinosaurs with horns and crests, spikes and razor-sharp claws. We are surrounded by dinosaurs: in museums, movies and theme parks, such as this display of robot dinosaurs in Japan. Even though they disappeared 65 million years ago, dinosaurs are "alive" in our imaginations. We are still learning about them; in fact, children today know more about dinosaurs than most adults do.

Ouranosaurus
Oo-ran-oh-sore-us:
"Brave reptile"
Group: plant eater
Period: early Cretaceous
Discovered: Africa, 1976
Size: 7 m (23 ft) long

Tyrannosaurus
Tie-ran-oh-sore-us:
"Tyrant lizard"
Group: meat eater
Period: late Cretaceous
Discovered: North America, 1905
Size: up to 14 m (46 ft)

Parasaurolophus
Par-ah-sore-ol-oh-fus:
"Parallel-sided reptile"
Group: plant eater
Period: late Cretaceous
Discovered: North America, 1923
Size: 10 m (33 ft) long

Triceratops
Try-ker-ah-tops:
"Three-horned face"
Group: plant eater
Period: late Cretaceous
Discovered: North America, 1889
Size: up to 9 m (30 ft)

Struthiomimus
Strooth-ee-oh-mime-us:
"Ostrich-mimic"
Group: meat eater
Period: late Cretaceous
Discovered: North America, 1917
Size: up to 4 m (13 ft)

53

— Dinosaur Facts —

Q Could dinosaurs swim?

A Although dinosaurs were not related to the giant marine reptiles, we know that at least some species could swim, and many of the plant eaters probably grazed in swamps. Scientists were puzzled by a set of *Diplodocus* footprints that showed only the animal's front feet. Then they realised the sauropod was floating in water, pushing itself along with its front feet and steering with its back legs and tail (as above).

Q How do you become a palaeontologist and dig up dinosaur fossils?

A To be a palaeontologist, you need to study science, especially biology and geology, at school and at university. You usually need a specialised research degree as well.

Q Where did dinosaurs live?

A Dinosaur fossils, and sometimes footprints, have been found on every continent, including Antarctica, which was not as cold during the Age of the Dinosaurs as it is today. Most parts of the world looked very different when the dinosaurs were alive. Slow geological changes have pushed up flat ground into steep mountains, and regions have become colder because continents have moved.

Q Did dinosaurs eat grass?

A No, because grasses did not evolve until the Miocene Epoch about 40 million years later than the dinosaurs.

Q Did any dinosaurs eat both meat and plants?

A Palaeontologists believe that some of the lizard-hipped dinosaurs, such as *Ornithomimus*, *Gallimimus* and *Struthiomimus*, probably ate small reptiles, mammals, insects—even other dinosaurs' eggs—as well as plants. Meat gave these gazelle-like animals the energy they needed to outrun predators. Speed was their only defence.

Q How can you tell a dinosaur's sex?

A It is very difficult to tell whether a dinosaur was male or female just from the bones. By looking at mammals, however, we can guess that male dinosaurs were generally larger than females, and it is likely that male duckbills (such as *Parasaurolophus* shown here) had larger crests. Fossils of *Pachycephalosaurus* show big differences in the size of the skull, and it seems that while both sexes had domed skulls, males had heavier heads for fighting, just like today's mountain goats.

Male

Female

Q Were dinosaurs affected by insects and parasites?

A Dinosaurs had thick, tough skins, but we are sure there were insects and ticks that bit them and sucked their blood—after all, today's crocodiles and monitor lizards are bitten by mosquitoes and blood-sucking flies. Although palaeontologists have never found fossils of parasites inside dinosaur bodies, it is likely that parasites attacked dinosaurs just as they do animals today.

Q Were meat-eating dinosaurs smarter than plant eaters?

A Yes, meat-eating dinosaurs had larger brains than plant eaters, and needed intelligence to hunt or ambush large and sometimes heavily armoured prey.

Q How long could dinosaurs live?

A Palaeontologists are unable to determine from fossil remains how long a dinosaur could live, but they do have some clues about how long it took dinosaurs to reach sexual maturity. Recent studies suggest that various dinosaurs such as hadrosaurs could breed somewhere between 5 and 12 years.

Q Why are fossil finds so exciting?

A They are incredibly rare. Some dinosaurs were the largest land animals ever to have lived on Earth, but large animals—whether they are reptiles or mammals—are not as common as small animals and their bones are therefore less likely to be found. Recently, the remains of many small dinosaurs were found in the Gobi Desert. But this was a very unusual find. Small animals can be torn apart by scavengers or eaten by insects. Their bones can be scattered by rain, or crushed by earth movements before they can become fossils. Even if these small bones are fossilised, they will be very hard to find and recognise millions of years later.

Q How many species of dinosaur were there?

A This is one question we will never be able to answer; only a few animals from any group are ever fossilised, so fossils give just a small "window" into the world of dinosaurs. About 800 species of dinosaur have been described but many of these may have been males and females from the same species and of different ages, so we probably know about only 350 genuine species of dinosaur. However, some scientists think there may have been between 1,000 and 1,300 species of dinosaur, while others estimate as many as 6,000 species.

Q Could dinosaurs sweat?

A No, their skin was scaly and did not have sweat glands, so they had other ways of keeping cool.

Q What do the names of dinosaurs mean ?

A The names of dinosaurs, like those of all animals and plants, tell us something about how each dinosaur is related to other dinosaurs. Names are made up from Latin and Greek words, and usually describe something outstanding about the animal. *Tyrannosaurus rex,* for example, means "king of the tyrant lizards"; *Corythosaurus* is "helmet lizard"; and *Protoceratops* stands for "first horned face".

Q Did prehistoric humans and dinosaurs live at the same time?

A Some movies may place humans and dinosaurs in the same prehistoric world, but humans evolved only 4 million years ago. This was 61 million years after the dinosaurs became extinct.

Index

Picture Credits

(t=top, b=bottom, l=left, r=right, c=centre, F=front, C=cover, B=back, Bg=background)
Ad-Libitum, 28cl, 39t (S. Bowey). American Museum of Natural History, 35cr (Neg. No. 35423/A.E. Anderson). Image Select, 50cl (Ann Ronan Picture Library). Ardea, 11tc (M.D. England), 36tcl, 54bl (F. Gohier). Auscape, 49br (Ferrero/Labat). Austral International, 36tc (Keystone). Australian Museum, 42c (C. Bento). Australian Picture Library, 51br (P. Menzel), 46cl (NASA/Reuters). Berlin Museum für Naturkunde, 48tc (P. Wellnhofer). Coo-ee Picture Library, 6cl (R. Ryan). Everett Collection, 51bl. The Image Bank, 47tr (J. Hunter), 46tl (Image Makers). Matrix, 48tl (Humboldt Museum, Berlin/L. Psihoyos), 20bl (The Natural History Museum, London/L. Psihoyos). 31cr, 43tr, 51bcr, 53tr (L. Psihoyos). The Natural History Museum, London, 11tr, 13tr, 22c, 22tl, 24/25b, 25c, 36cl, 36tl, 38bl, 42bl. NHPA, 42tcl (P. Johnson). David Norman, 50bl. The Photo Library, Sydney, 33tc (SPL/S. Stammers). Planet Earth Pictures, 48cl (P. Chapman), 42tl (W. Dennis). Stock

Photos, 49bcr (Animals Animals). Tom Stack & Associates, 11tl (J. Cancalosi). University of Chicago Hospitals, 14bl.

Illustration Credits

Wendy de Paauw, 50/51t. Simone End, 4/5c, 5br, 9brc, 10tl, 17r, 19c, 19t, 22tl, 25tr, 27cr, 29cr, 29tl, 35bc, 37ct, 40tl, 41c, 41ct, 41tl, 41tr, 51c, 52/53c, 54, 55c, icons. Christer Eriksson, 20/21c, 26/27c, 31c, 44/45c, 46/47c, 48/49c. John Francis/Bernard Thornton Artists, UK, 14/15c, 16/17c, 18/19c. David Kirshner, 2/3b, 10bc, 10bl, 11bl, 11br, 11tc, 22/23c, 28/29c, 35tr, 42/43c, 42b, 47br, 49bl. Frank Knight, 5cr, 6bc, 13cr, 20cl, 23tr, 24bc, 27br, 29cr, 31br, 32tl, 33r, 34, 34/35tc/35tr, 41br, 44, 45ct, 45tl, 48bl. James McKinnon, 1, 8/9c, 8tl, 20tl, 24/25t, 24tr, 25br, 25c, 29b, 32/33b, 36/37b. Colin Newman/Bernard Thornton Artists, UK, 4tl, 6/7c, 7t, 12/13b, 12tl, 13tl, 38/39c, 38ct, 38tl, 39cr. Paul Newman, 47cr. Marilyn Pride, 15bc.

Peter Schouten, 2tl, 4b, 5t, 15r, 17t, 19b, 21tr, 22bl, 23br, 26bl, 27tr, 30, 31t, 40/41c. Ray Sim, 14tl, 16tl, 18tl, 33t. Rod Westblade, endpapers.

Cover Credits

Christer Eriksson, FCc. Peter Schouten, FCtr, BCtl. Colin Newman/Bernard Thornton Artists, UK, FCtl. Frank Knight, BCbr. Quarto Publishing, Bg.